T0152079

15

A WRIGLEY BOOK
about

STRENGTH

BY DENIS WRIGLEY

A strong bridge?

but not strong enough!

Some people are strong

and some are weak.

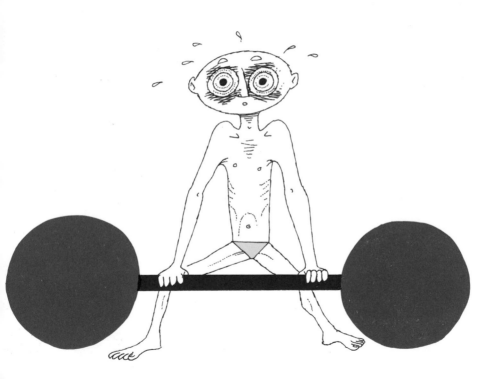

Some people can lift
heavy things. . . .

and some people find it difficult!

It depends on the problem

and the power to solve it.

A strong rope
to lift a heavy weight.

A strong horse
to pull a heavy load.

A strong runner
to win the race.

A strong scent
carried on the breeze.

A strong will helps you
to stop eating
too many sweets. . . .

but a weak will
may make you greedy!!

Eyesight is also sometimes weak.

Other words show strength and weakness.

A FRAGILE jug breaks easily.

A POWERFUL motor boat
travels fast.

A FEEBLE plant needs support.

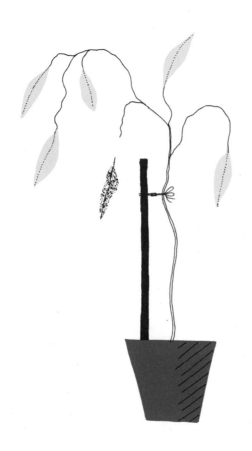

Strength needs testing
but be careful
how you do it!

First published 1976
Copyright © 1976 Denis Wrigley
ISBN 07188 2187 4
Printed in Hong Kong

The Wrigley Books

Published by
LUTTERWORTH PRESS • GUILDFORD AND LONDON

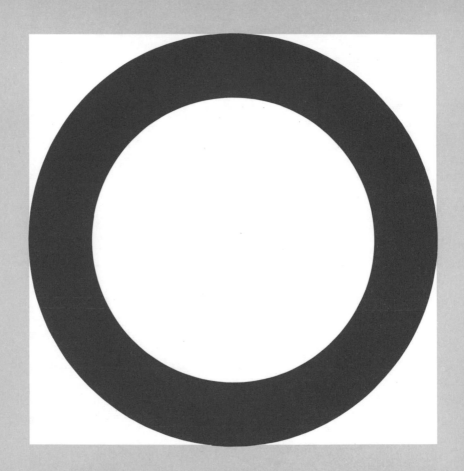